# How to Sell Annuities.
# Second Edition

Annuity Sales Techniques, Tips and Strategies.

By Michael Bonilla, CPCU

**Copyright 2019**

About the Author.

Believe it or not this section is always the hardest for me to write about. I really don't enjoy talking about myself. I enjoy having people talk about themselves. What do people want to know about an author? Background? Experiences? Belief systems? I enjoy breaking things and putting them back together. What kind of person am I? What kind of person do I want to represent?

Let me tell you a brief story that tells you what kind of person I am. Back in the early 90's I was sketching out my design for a boxcar derby car for boy scouts. This was my first race and I couldn't think of the type of car I wanted to build. To say the least there was zero inspiration. I scribbled out some designs on this piece of paper and eventually after running out of paper went into the den to find more paper. I stopped for a second and glanced over by the window. After staring out of the window for a second (maybe several minutes) I saw my father as he was pulling into the driveway with his 1990 White Dodge diesel, you could hear it for miles.

Then it hit me. What if I used his truck as the design? I re-read the instructions and rules for the derby. The boxcar kit came in a small cardboard box with a block of wood we could use to make our cars. The instructions read as follows:

* Must have 4 wheels
* Must weigh X LBs, no more and no less.
* Must be X inches long by X Inches wide.

So, that being said. Nowhere in the rules/instructions did it specifically say "this boxcar must be a car". So, for the first time in the boxcar derby history. Michael Bonilla entered a truck. To which everyone started laughing. It was a small wooded version of a 1990's Dodge Ram 2500. With a big Pepsi decal on the driver side door. So, we called it the Pepsi truck.

I placed my 'car' on the race line for the first race and hoped for the best. The judges looked at it. It met the weight requirements, the size requirements and had the appropriate amount of wheels. So, we raced and I waited with anticipation for the results.

As I was short I couldn't even see the race. All I heard was, "Pepsi truck 1st place." After all 5 races that day I kept hearing those same words over and over again.

After sweeping that year's event. The following year I decided to change it up and make a replica of the Mach 5 Speed Racer Car, in which I came in third place. That next year every 'car' was a truck, besides mine. Don't bend the rules, don't break the rules, test the rules and test the boundaries of the game you are given. Look for loopholes and exploits in the system.

I'm unsure what kind of insight that might have provided. Nevertheless, this book is the longest, most through and probably well thought out I have written to date. I'm an author, a consultant, a former agency owner, an avid golfer, a husband and most importantly someone who enjoys giving back through teaching.

## Acknowledgments

I'd like to take some time to acknowledge all of my dedicated readers and all of the readers that have left invaluable feedback. I take your reviews seriously and use them to make adjustments to my process and my writing style. Previously, I spent more time on content, somewhat of a form over function kind of thinking. From your feedback I have made content changes, and also have made changes to the structure of my books. I look forward to hearing your thoughts and reading your reviews. Thanks again for leaving me with your thoughts as I develop my own.

## Preface

In this second edition of "How to Sell Annuities" you will find additional insight, tips, useful questions and statistics to help you drive you practice. Writing this second edition it was clear that there was more I could contribute and the resulting new edition should be a significant improvement over the first draft. Annuities are what some industry analysts would consider the 'drug' of our industry, why? Because, once you sell your first annuity most agents never want to sell anything else. So, that being said, how can this book help your annuity sales? I'm looking for you to partake with one critical piece of information, whether that is a new strategy for selling, understanding how to improve your workflow/process and or some kind of inspiration for prospecting.

*"Annuities are not usually bought they are sold."* - Unknown

## Contents

About the Author. ....................................................................4

Acknowledgments .................................................................7

Preface. ..................................................................................8

Chapter 1: Introduction........................................................16

    What do you do really well?............................................20

    Key Takeaways from this book........................................21

    The 'Aha Moment' and the Insurance Epiphany .....22

    Let's talk expectations....................................................23

Chapter 2: Fundamental Sales Tips ...................................26

    Rule Number 1: Don't Complicate Something Simple. ...........................................................................26

    Rule Number 2: Always be agreeable. .........................27

    Rule Number 3: Understand the Person.....................28

    Rule Number 4: The Prospect Needs to understand you....................................................................................30

    Rule Number 5: Reciprocity ...........................................30

    Rule Number 6: Stick to a process. ..............................31

    Rule Number 7: Know When To Close and Know When to Fold. ..................................................................33

    Rule Number 8: Ask Open Ended Questions............35

    Rule number 9: Set Expectations..................................36

    Rule Number 10: Don't lose control of the conversation. ......................................................................36

    Rule Number 11: Don't always try to reinvent the wheel. ..................................................................................38

    Rule Number 12: Speak in Future Tense ....................39

Rule Number 13: Ask for Permission to Ask for the Sale .................................................................................. 39

Rule Number 14: Don't Present Price Present a Solution. ............................................................................. 40

Rule Number 15: Put yourself in a position to win. ...................................................................................... 41

Rule Number 16: Dance through the pain ................ 41

Rule Number 17: Have a Personal Story ................... 41

Chapter 3: What is an Annuity? ........................................ 44

How does an Annuity work? ........................................ 44

Types of Annuities ....................................................... 45

Understanding Two Strategies .................................... 45

Strategy 1: Equity Indexed Annuity ............................ 46

Strategy 2: Immediate Annuity to Fund a Life/LTC. ................................................................................... 47

General Annuity Questions .......................................... 48

    Mike, can I roll my qualified plan (401K, IRA, Roth, ETC) into an annuity? ........................................ 48

    What are the tax implications? ............................... 48

    Is there a distribution tax penalty if I roll over before age 59? ........................................................... 49

Chapter 4: Which Clients are suited for Annuities? ... 51

Textbook Suitability ..................................................... 51

Target Market ............................................................... 52

Indexed Annuity Qualifiers/Needs .............................. 53

Immediate Annuity Qualifiers ..................................... 53

But Mike, is health of the annuitant a concern? ..... 54

Chapter 5: Marketing Annuities? ............................................. 56
   But Mike, How can we use this information? ........... 58
   Find a Mentor and a Coach ............................................. 60
Chapter 6: Annuity Strategy Overview ........................... 63
   Stage 1: Prospecting ....................................................... 63
   Stage 2: Fact Finding & Qualifying .............................. 64
   Stage 3: Product Presentation & Close ..................... 66
   Stage 4: Follow Up ........................................................... 67
Chapter 7: Areas of Concerns for Retirees ................... 69
   3 Concerns/Challenges that face every Retired Person ................................................................................ 69
   Median Retirement Savings by Age in the USA ...... 71
Chapter 8: 3 Primary Sources of Retirement Income ................................................................................................ 74
   Understand Social Security and potential pitfalls. .74
   Why Annuities compliment Social Security in a retirement plan. ................................................................ 75
   Qualified Plan or Pension Plan ..................................... 76
   Why do people have money in their savings account? ............................................................................. 77
   What emergency expenses would you need to use your savings for? ............................................................. 77
Chapter 9: How Annuities can fill the gap for a retiree. ...................................................................................... 80
   Qualifying Process ........................................................... 80
   Selling Yourself. ................................................................ 82
   Analyze Current Retirement Plan ................................ 82

Explain/address the Areas of Concern. ..................83
Fill the Gaps / Design a Plan ..............................84
But Mike, what if the client does not have Life Insurance and or does not have long term care insurance?......................................................84
Tax Advantages of this strategy? ........................84
Major Downsides of this plan. .............................85
But Mike, if we are selling peace of mind how do we justify the drawbacks? .....................................85
Case Study Client Example ................................86
Address Possible Objections ...............................89
Building a Fact Finder.........................................90
Pro's and Cons of Annuities ................................93
    The Argument for Annuities................................94
    The Argument against Annuities........................94

Chapter 10: Dealing with External Stakeholders .......97
    The Triple A's ................................................97
    "I need to speak with my husband/wife/spouse.".98
    Flipping the Script..........................................99

Chapter 11: Understanding Stats........................103
    Life Statistics..............................................104
    Retirement Statistics ...................................105

Disclaimer .......................................................107
Index of Questions ...........................................108
Summation ......................................................110

*"Quality is not an act, it is a habit."*

*- Aristotle*

## Chapter 1: Introduction

If there is a single take away from this book, remember this, selling insurance is a process. It's a process that is a both an art and a science. What does it take to sell annuities and life insurance? One question, how well can you hold a conversation? That being said, every sale no matter how unique the client the overall process remains more or less the same. People tend to give you the same objections and tend to walk along similar lines of thinking.

Whether you are a seasoned insurance veteran or a new entry, this book might be just what you're looking for. I'd like to think that there are golden nuggets of wisdom in this book. If you find something useful, use it. If you don't discard it. Some of this book is going to be academic, so of it theoretical and some of it highly practical.

Selling an Annuity requires a somewhat

different approach when you compare it to other insurance products. An annuity is really an investment vehicle that is an insurance product. Unlike, a life policy that is a life insurance product that can be an investment vehicle.

Purchasing life insurance or in this case an annuity isn't like purchasing a bar of soap at the grocery store. There should be a good amount of consideration and thought that comes along with the purchase.

Applying for insurance is a lot like applying for a job. Do you always get every job that you apply for? Are you guaranteed to get the job? Insurance is exclusive by its very discriminatory nature, there is a qualification and selection process.

It's also unique in that it is something you have to qualify for. As a professional take the time to learn your product and your craft. It's easy to get an insurance license but when we talk about retirement planning we are talking about people's money.

Have you ever heard people say that life insurance and annuities are an emotional sale? The key difference from what separates a great life agent and a price driven life agent is the ability to tether a life insurance policy or in this case annuities with personal experiences of the insured. How do you make this policy meaningful to the prospect?

This business has always been a relationship business and for the foreseeable future that should remain relatively true. Of course, this is easier said than done. So, in this book we will cover how to evoke those emotions, understanding clients and developing value based sales approaches.

That being said don't force ideas on people, just give them something to think about and they will arrive at the same conclusion. This is why question asking is the foundation to successful sales, because it forces prospects to think and grapple with ideas.

As you read this book I want you to begin to think about selling in a different light. Selling is a lot like Texas Hold'em. Poker is classified as a limited information game. Which means each hand you are granted limited information to make a decision. Each hand has what are called implied odds. Just like in selling people are not always open books. You have to take time to 'read' them and understand what they care about. You have X amount of information and you have to make a decision. How you process that info will determine for the most part the outcome of a sale. This is why understanding each client on an individual level is so important. Understanding and addressing their concerns and questions and overall understanding what they need and what they want.

My favorite poker player is Daniel Negreanu.

The reason why he is my favorite poker player is the fact that he is a talker. By talking he is able to read people and get information that isn't on the board. Like they say in poker, play the player across from you not the hand.

As an Agent our job is to help clients make educated and informed decisions. So, how do we do that? We have to see what cards everyone is playing with. Figure out why the person is looking to buy, find out if there are gaps in the current plan, find out if the person is a think or feel person and find out what the person cares about.

What do you do really well?

What do you do really well? When I first started writing this was the central premise for all of my books. It's a question that I like to ask referral partners, other agents and anyone who talks to me for more than five minutes of time. It a question that gives me immediate insight into the person I'm dealing with. It's a question that either exposes or empowers a salesperson.

Why is this question so powerful? Because, if you can't answer this question at any time, then how can we reasonable expect the client to answer on your behalf. How can we expect a referral partner to talk you up when insurance springs up in the topic of conversation? As you read this book, please ask yourself this question and make sure to come up with your answer.

Key Takeaways from this book

- How do I know when a client is a good annuity candidate?
- Where do I find the money?
- Where do I find the potential clients?
- How do I pitch the concept?
- Qualifying questions

- Who should be involved in the conversation?
- Arguments for Annuities
- Arguments Against Annuities

The 'Aha Moment' and the Insurance Epiphany

At some point in the insurance buying process the insured has to arrive at what I like to call an inflexion point in their decision making. They either have to make a decision to take or not take your proposal, but really they have to make a decision to protect their assets or leave their assists exposed to risk. At some point in my presentation, when selling any type of insurance, they (the client) have to seriously consider the negative ramifications of not signing up. This is why we plant seeds during the presentation and illustrate the risk of either choice. Are job is not to scare someone into making an informed decision, but to lay out the options with an ethical framework that demonstrates how the proposal is in the best interest of the client. What happens if you don't protect your family against financial devastation? What happens if you decline life insurance coverage, walk out of this office and get hit by a bus?

Let's talk expectations.

This book is not a one size fits all annuity closers guide to every possible situation. My goal with this book is not to tell you how to think or tell you what to think, but my goal is to give you something to think about. This book was developed to help you enable yourself in overall strategy development and thoughtful sales techniques. How can we arrange a conversation in a way that will help you move the dial in your annuity sales? Most readers of this book are probably looking for ways to get into annuity sales and find ways to pursue annuity sales. Every time I read an insurance book or sales book in general, I am looking for one great idea. In this book I'd like to hope I can pass on to you one great idea.

*"You must understand fear so you can manipulate it. Fear is like fire. You can make it work for you; it can warm you in the winter, cook your food when you're hungry, give you light when you're in the dark and produce energy. Let it go out of control and it can hurt you, even kill you...fear is a friend of exceptional people."* **– Cus D'Amato**

## Chapter 2: Fundamental Sales Tips

Learning isn't easy. I hate studying, but it's essential to growth. Every month I pick up at least one new sales book to read. Why? Because, I might pick up that million dollar idea or that new pitch or a new angle to adapt my process. In this part of the book we are going to take a general approach to selling and then later on in the book take a microscope and be very specific with regards to our approach. Whether you consider yourself a veteran salesperson or a newbie, take some time here and digest these tips. Think about why these tips are useful, or find reasons why you feel they are useless and think about them.

Rule Number 1: Don't Complicate Something Simple.

Rule number one of selling insurance is to keep it simple and to the point. We are selling insurance not building a space ship. Most consumers don't know what they don't know. Most consumers don't know what they have, what they need, what they're current risk profile looks like and what they are missing out on. Explain the concepts in digestible terms that consumers can actually understand and stray away from using too much insurance jargon.

About 5 years ago or so, I had the misfortune of sitting through a long-winded sales consultation with a life agent appointed by one of the world's largest life insurance companies. The life agent had a well thought out, but thoroughly confusing Indexed Universal Life Presentation. After about 45 minutes of this rep carrying on I started wondering if she actually was going to stop talking and listen.

Rule Number 2: Always be agreeable.

Selling is as much an art as it is a science. There is no formula for agreeableness, some people are naturally more agreeable than others. Just know that the more confrontational we are as salespeople the worse your odds are for closing a sale. The first person to agree is generally the one that is going to have the advantage during the negotiating process. When we agree we are changing the language of the typical sales process, in that, this is not going to be an 'I'm right and you're wrong' type of conversation. This conversation is going to be a collaborative experience.

### Rule Number 3: Understand the Person.

Don't make snap judgements about what someone can afford. Dig. Take the time to ask questions and understand the person sitting across the table. One day a 'surfer dude' walked into my office, dressed in shorts, a Tommy B shirt, shades on the back of his head, tattered sandals and enough wrist bands to make Johnny Depp envious. What was he looking for? This surfer dude was looking for auto insurance and brought in his Dec page. Now, what would most people assume at this point? Well, clearly he is a candidate for 15/30 state minimum limits, right? Wrong! Turns out his current Dec page did have 15/30, but I started digging the same way I would have for an advanced markets case.

Turns out this surfer dude, who did in fact surf, was also in need of some better insurance. Great, do you own or rent? Currently, he was renting an apartment. So, tell me about the apartment, to which he replied, it's all right. Okay, what do you do for a living? To which he replied, 'I'm an artist.' When I started digging a little further into what that meant, it turns out to my surprise that this gentleman restored art in the ball park of $7,000,000 to $15,000,000 pieces of classical artwork. All of which he kept in his home. Now, how does a person like this get 15/30? According to the prospect, turned client, no one ever bothered to have the conversation with him. Everyone assumed he needed state minimums because his current Dec page had state minimums.

Rule Number 4: The Prospect Needs to understand you.

Ask yourself does the prospect have enough information to know, like and trust me? According to Bob Berg all things being equal this is the determining ethos people use for selecting whom to do business with. If not, then you need to build that trust through conversation. Why should this person do business with and not the other guy down the street?

Rule Number 5: Reciprocity

If an insurance sale is a search for the truth we need to follow the rule of reciprocity. The rule of reciprocity makes the insurance buying process a collaborative effort not a confrontational one. Follow a simple rule of thumb, give before you get.

Remember you make no money until the

person signs up with you, so you are educating them for free. This is the key to reciprocity. You ask questions to evoke emotions during the process and client has questions that you answer to provide certainty.

### Rule Number 6: Stick to a process.

One of my friends had something in her eye and she kept rubbing it to no avail. I passed onto her a simple process I learned, 'close your eye and drag your find down the top and up the bottom halves of your lids, like a windshield wiper.' It's a process that I learned and actually works rather well. To which she replied, 'you have a process for everything.' That didn't used to be the case, I used to be the sales guy who was all personality and energy. This is an overrated sales style that most novice salespeople cling to.

Every person is different, but every sale is

exactly the same. In that, people give you the same responses, the same objections and will follow a path. When you start selling insurance it's important to remember that you have a start, you build rapport, you ask questions that are open ended, you find a problem if one exists, and you build a solution/close.

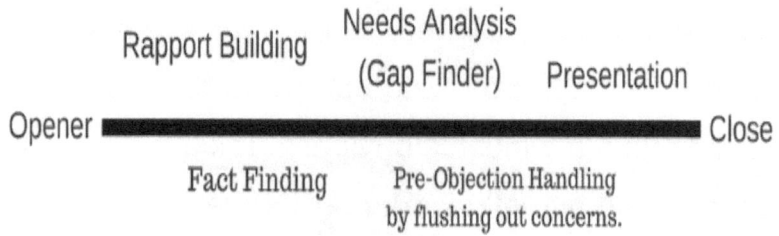

There are two types of people that sit in front of you. There are think type of people and feel type of people. What I mean is that people respond to questions in different ways. Some people say, "I think…" and some people say, "I feel…"

The reason why you need to grasp this concept, is the fact that during a sale we have these invisible boundaries. Emotional or feel people require stories and think people require figures and facts. Not everyone is the same. But, there is a limit for feel people and there is a limit for think people that we have to monitor in the sales process.

> Rule Number 7: Know When To Close and Know When to Fold.

Some prospects believe it or not just enjoy talking to sales people and have no intention of buying. Being a salesperson you must think that is somewhat crazy, I did. But, it's true. During your presentation it's important to know when people are giving off buying signals and asking buying questions. Why? Because, that will give you a strong indication of when someone is ready to be closed.

Think of a sale like a Turkey in the oven. First you have to marinate the turkey. Then you preheat the oven. After your prep work is complete and the oven is at the right temperature you put the Turkey in the oven. Some turkeys require more prep work because some are FROZEN and some are fresh. You cook the turkey and check the temperature along the way. But, you have to keep marinating the turkey as it cooks. If the internal temperature is correct after X amount of hours you pull it out and it's moist. If you leave it in too long it dries out or maybe even burns or becomes ruined.

I'll make an effort to dispense with the food analogies for the rest of the book. Think of it this way. Think of it like an index. The 'Closability' index. Some people are easier to close than others and some require a tremendous amount of effort. But, either way the prospect will ask buying questions.

Well, what's a buying question? For instance, "How much does this cost?" If you are not interested in a product you do not ask how much it will cost. Simple.

### Rule Number 8: Ask Open Ended Questions

If you are new to sales or new to insurance. Your best friend is the ability to ask open ended questions and leading questions. Would you mind if we talked about open ended questions? This is a directive question asking for permission to ask a question. How do you feel about annuity sales? What do you think about annuity sales? Whatever the answer always remember to ask follow up questions. You have two ears and one mouth so as a ratio ask too questions before you start to babble on about insurance.

## Rule number 9: Set Expectations

Like in any relationship you need to set boundaries. What should a client come to expect of you? What do you expect of a client? A lot of Agents (including myself) tell a client that they meet with each client once per year to make sure the insurance is current or on target. There is nothing customized about that statement for a client. Instead why not just ask. How often would you like to meet each year to discuss your insurance? Most of my clients find once a year to meet their needs but some prefer a call once a quarter to check in.

## Rule Number 10: Don't lose control of the conversation.

Probably the most common challenge for newer agents is not maintaining focus. A prospect is going to focus on price if you let them and it can derail the conversation.

Price is merely the cost of value. It's your job to educate and present the value. Remember you are the expert and what you focus on will direct the conversation. Don't avoid talking about price, but at the same time don't rush or lead with price. See Diagram Below.

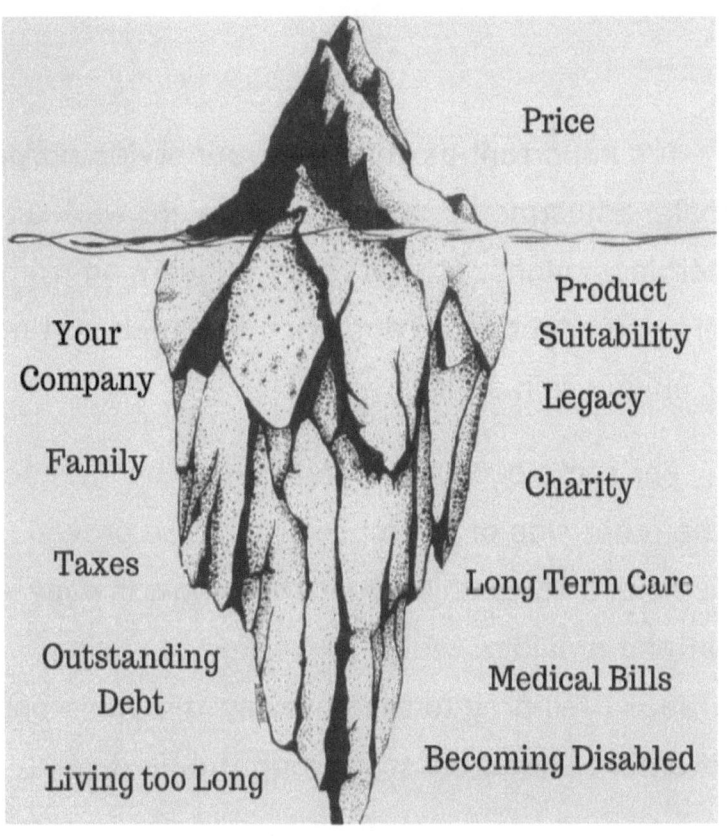

Rule Number 11: Don't always try to reinvent the wheel.

My father was a carpenter and used to say the nail that sticks out tends to get hammered. Craft your approach as you learn your trade. If your trade is selling insurance, then read, apply and learn.

It's important as you craft your style/approach to make adjustments. Somethings might work and somethings might not. But, start by learning from others and adopting an approach and then putting your unique spin on it.

For some people the grass is always greener on the other side of the fence. There are proven systems and sales techniques that you can copy, adopt and emulate. When I first started selling insurance I fell prey to the 'my-way-is-always-better' syndrome, I like to call it learning the hard way.

Rule Number 12: Speak in Future Tense

Learn to speak in the future tense. As your Agent... fill in the blank statement. While I was going to college I paid my way by being a Personal Trainer. I learned very quickly to speak in the assumptive future tense. As your blank... here's how I can be of service to you. "Well, I haven't said I would sign up with you yet." This is the response I want to hear from a client, a soft objection or they might ask buying questions and be able to be closed on the spot. I'm planting seeds not seeds of doubt. But, planting a picture in their head to so some thinking. Picturing in their head how working with me is going to look like and benefit them.

Rule Number 13: Ask for Permission to Ask for the Sale

This is by far my favorite rule and the most overlooked by most insurance salespeople. Along time ago my great grandfather taught me, 'to never open a man's (families) refrigerator without asking for permission.' Why? Because, it's rude among other reasons that might not be as culturally relevant in today's society. When selling make sure to ask for permission to ask for the sale. What I mean is that prior to presenting make sure to ask if it's okay to present a solution. Put some curiosity in there, check the rapport and ask for permission. Don't force your sales pitch on someone.

### Rule Number 14: Don't Present Price Present a Solution.

New salespeople present themselves, because they don't know any better other than to be eager, overzealous, and enthusiastic. Transactional salespeople present on price and only price as the focus. Relationship based salespeople present a product that comes with them as the center piece of value. Consultative sales people present a product and focus on coverage needs. The best salespeople present a solution to a problem and the insurance is vehicle to fulfill the problem/solution dynamic.

Rule Number 15: Put yourself in a position to win.

Often we try to sell anyone who can fog a mirror. It happens. The hardest lesson to learn as an agent is that not everyone is a customer. People who walk into your office might not be qualified to buy what you are offering. Don't put yourself into a position to fail by trying to qualify and sell everyone. Remember learning about the gold rush? Prospectors sat in rivers sifting through dirt, swirling water in a dish to find flakes of gold. What they were not trying to do was turn that dirt into gold.

Rule Number 16: Dance through the pain

Persistency is the number one indicator of longevity for a salesperson. Roughly, 97% of life insurance agents and financial advisors fail in the first year. Why? Persistency. We get constantly rejected, again and again. It's not easy to bounce back up and will yourself to keep going.

Rule Number 17: Have a Personal Story

Having a personal story can make or break

your sales presentation. If you don't have a compelling reason for doing what you do, sales becomes infinitely more challenging. After witnessing the 'great recession' I had family members lose 50% of their 401k's and qualified plans, almost overnight. What would have happened if they took immediate annuities on their 401k's? They wouldn't have lost a dime. Now granted a lot of that value was regained, but it took 10 years! Imagine waiting to liquidate your life savings for ten years into your retirement.

*"Experience alone does not create knowledge."* –
**Kurt Lewin**

## Chapter 3: What is an Annuity?

In this book we are going to cover a lot of ground. We are going to talk about the ins and outs of annuity sales. We are going to cover how Annuities work, which clients annuities are suited for, strategies to sell annuities and much more. The first question we have to ask is how does an Annuity work.

### How does an Annuity work?

If a life insurance product is designed to create an estate when a person dies, an annuity simply is there to liquidate and add to an estate while a person is a live. Generally speaking an annuity is a tax deferred insurance product where you give the life insurance company X amount of dollars starting around $10,000.

The life insurance company will invest your

money and pay you a certain percentage of interest in return for a lump sum. There are surrender charges, possible riders and death benefit components for some annuities.

*Note from Author: This book is sales focused more than product focused. If you have specific annuity product questions make sure to ask your TPA or insurance company.*

## Types of Annuities

For the purposes of this book we are going to talk about two kinds of annuities, Equity Indexed and Immediate Annuities with Guaranteed Payments for life.

## Understanding Two Strategies

Selling insurance is a rather easy endeavor, it

requires that you talk to enough people and say the right things. How do we learn to walk? Baby steps... I'm a firm believer in learning a couple strategies really well, as opposed to learning a little about a bunch of strategies. The best way to learn how to sell Annuities is by learning two simple strategies and building from there. Once you have learned those two strategies learn two products that can fit client's needs within those strategies. This will also prevent you trying to be a jack of all trade and master of none.

## Strategy 1: Equity Indexed Annuity

Annuities in my approximation are great vehicles for clients with highly conservative investment appetites and investment goals with minimal risk. The first and easiest Annuity strategy to learn is simply how to sell an Indexed Annuity. Both strategy involves to some extent addressing key areas of concern during retirement (discussed later) and leveraging money sitting in savings accounts. When you keep money in a Savings Account it's earning a negative return on investment. Why? Because, inflation is around 3% and a bank account pays out around 0.01% to 0.05 APY. Why would you let your money lose money? For this strategy, just learn and understand Indexed Annuities. This strategy is a standalone annuity that is replacing money the client just plans on sitting around in a savings account for an extended time horizon. It's simple and it's merely an 'all-in' style approach for 5 to 10 years.

Usually Annuities to be effective require large lump sums to fund. Keeping that in mind the first strategy is selling the safety and security of an indexed annuity with a 5 to 10 year time horizon. This strategy works great assuming the person doesn't have any immediate liquidation needs.

Strategy 2: Immediate Annuity to Fund a Life/LTC.

The second strategy is somewhat more complex. The second strategy involved selling an immediate annuity and leveraging the income to purchase a permanent life insurance policy to match the amount of money put into the annuity and then add a disability/LTC rider or purchase a standalone LTC policy. Basically, you can leverage the income into purchasing two other life products and still have money left over for additional income.

### General Annuity Questions

Mike, can I roll my qualified plan (401K, IRA, Roth, ETC) into an annuity?

Yes, it is possible. A qualified plan and even a conventional pension plan can be rolled into a tax-free annuity.

What are the tax implications?

Depending on the roll over this can be done without any tax penalty as the money is transferred into a holding account and then invested in the annuity. **Consult an attorney and your CPA.**

Is there a distribution tax penalty if I roll over before age 59?

The IRS will allow this type of roll over without assessing a penalty, generally speaking. Now, that doesn't mean you will avoid taxes. When you invest in an immediate annuity there will be income earned and taxes due on that income.

*Because your own strength is unequal to the task, do not assume that it is beyond the powers of man; but if anything is within the powers and province of man, believe that it is within your own compass also.*
**Marcus Aurelius**

## Chapter 4: Which Clients are suited for Annuities?

This question is somewhat open ended. Because, the truth is when it comes to retirement planning there is no one size fits all plan of attack that works for everyone in every situation. I think the real question we all have to ask is, "How adverse is the retiree/client to the idea of losing money/risk." Most retired people have a lower risk tolerance, especially if they have six figures stashed away in a bank account collecting dust.

### Textbook Suitability

If you were on the flipside of the coin and shopping for an annuity. How would you find it suitable? Here is what the **2010 NAIC model regulation** says to consider, "...*the insurer or insurance producer shall have reasonable grounds for believing that the recommendation to purchase an annuity or exchange an annuity is suitable for the consumer based on the facts disclosed by the* *consumer as to his or her investments and other insurance products and financial situation and needs, including the consumer's suitability information."*

Also, the NAIC model requires us to have a reasonable basis for believing the consumer would benefit from certain features of the annuity and that any underlying subaccounts are suitable for the client.

### Target Market

**Target Market 1**: People with large sums of money sitting around in bank accounts or financially conservative retirees or pre-retirees.

**Target Market 2**: People who already have an interest in long term care insurance. Why? Because, if there is an interest in long term care insurance that tells me there is money to protect, otherwise there is rarely any interest given the cost of LTC.

**Target Market 3**: Pre-retired Pensioners

### Indexed Annuity Qualifiers/Needs

For an indexed strategy or immediate income strategy the following are usually important 'needs' of a retired person:

- Not running out of money.
- Principal Protection
- Preservation of Capital
- Having Something to Leave Behind
- Complimenting Social Security
- Hedging Against Loss

### Immediate Annuity Qualifiers

- Money Sitting Around
- Conservative Investment Desired
- No Need for Use of Large Sum of Money
- Wants to hedge against market risk

- Cares about capital preservation over interest rate

But Mike, is health of the annuitant a concern?

Yes, it's the primary concern depending on the strategy you choose to implement. Remember, an annuity contract does have life insurance components and health should always be a factor to consider and that the client carefully considers before purchasing an annuity.

*"If everyone is thinking alike, then somebody isn't thinking."* – **George Patton**

## Chapter 5: Marketing Annuities?

Annuities are not usually bought they are sold. Is that my opinion or is that fact? Well, according to LifeHappens.com and other industry sites, '70% of purchasers are prompted by an agent to get a quote.' So, where do we look for buyers? Let's break down the key annuity purchaser demographics. So, what do we need to know when marketing annuities? First, we have to find people in or near retirement. Second, we have to find people with money sitting around.

The **2013 Survey of Owners of Individual Annuity Contracts** found some interesting statistics to start our search for buyers. The research found that the Age at which First Annuity was purchased was as follows:

- Under 50 years old 39%.
- 50 to 64 years old 47%.
- 65 years and older 14%.

The study also found that the majority of individual annuity owners were in fact female, but only slightly.

Furthermore, the study found that among annuity owners.

- 58% were Married
- 24% were Widowed
- 10% were Single Never Married
- 7% were Divorced.

The study found that among owners their employment status was as follows:

- 65% Retired.
- 20% Employed Full Time
- 8% Employed Part Time.
- 3% Homemaker.
- 4% Other.

The last point I want to pick out of that study was that it found Household Income to be as such:

- 5% Under $20,000
- 16% $20,000 to $39,999
- 14% $40,000 to 49,999
- 25% $50,000 to $74,999
- 20% $75,000 to $99,999
- 13% 100,000 to $199,999
- 7% $200,0000

This shows that the average premium on an annuity is around $60,000 and 60% of annuity owners make less than $74,999 combined adjusted gross income. Which would basically equate to a family both working part time or close to full time.

But Mike, How can we use this information?

Success leaves clues. So, that being said, we are looking for pre-retirees between the ages of 50 to 65, who are married or single and a majority of these people are making less than $75,000 in household income. Think of a few places where you might find those people, in large groups. Also, remember we are looking for people with an excess of $50,000 in savings and with a target premium of over $100,000 in savings.

The first thing that comes to my mind would be a mobile home park. Granted I realize how that comes off, but it fits the parameter of what the study found. More importantly it's an untapped and underserved community of people that could use your expertise and advice. Help the underserved and it will usually reap rewards.

Believe it or not, according to the Washington Post, there are 18 Million people living in mobile home parks in America. If we assume that the average age is around 50 years old, average family size of 2 and a savings per family of $20,000, we can safely say there is around $18 to $20 Billion dollars in potential annuities.

*Remember, with insurance it's important to*

*focus on base hits and not just homeruns. If you have the market for those households that earn $200,000+ then go for it. But, if you can pick up a $60,000 annuity each month, then go for it.*

For me as a rule of thumb, I always go where others are not. I go into a space and try to dominate that space. Before you start running around to mobile homes pitching annuities make sure you check with Department of insurance regulations and your TPA for adequacy.

### Find a Mentor and a Coach

I've always been a fast study, because I like breaking things and putting them back together. Probably, due to my childhood obsession with Legos or tinker toys. When I first jumped over to the independent side of the business, let me tell you there was quite a learning curve. There is a smidgen of crossover, but they are two different animals all together. From a life and annuities perspective, I had to teach myself from scratch and with no management team support or up line or district manager.

So, finding a mentor was crucial for my own development and success in the industry. I sought out countless great salespeople, books, articles, forums and mentors. I spoke with every insurance agent and their brother if it could help me move policies. Don't feel ashamed to ask for someone's help, this was the most valuable lesson I learned. Putting my pride aside and asking for help, this to me was an invaluable way to approach my practice. Why? Because, there was no way starting as a scratch broker that I possibly knew all the answers, and I still do not presume that I know all the answers.

"The essence of strategy is choosing what not to do."
Michael Porter

## Chapter 6: Annuity Strategy Overview

In this chapter we are going to breakdown the component parts of the annuity sales life cycle. This chapter is meant as a general framework for the overall annuity sales process and later on in the book we will go into some more detail. The four stages we will cover are:

Stage 1: Prospecting

Stage 2: Fact Finding Expedition and Qualifying Meeting

Stage 3: Product Presentation

Stage 4: Follow Up

### Stage 1: Prospecting

Prospecting is the life blood of any agency. As agents we need to speak with enough people and say the right things to those people. When prospecting remember not to always swing for the fences and try to force a homerun. I'm not saying avoid going for the big fish, but more so to focus on getting on base. If you sell a $10,000 annuity, it's not going to make your rich, but at the same time that single annuity sale might result in 3 or 4 new referrals. During the prospecting phase we are simply getting someone's attention.

## Stage 2: Fact Finding & Qualifying

What is our job in stage 2? We want to qualify, gather information about the prospect, and develop the interest of the prospect. This is the point where we develop initial interest and buy-in. We can also use this time to educate, but be vary of throwing too much at the prospect.

- Fact Finder / Fact Sheet
- Rapport Building
- Determine Goals

- Determine Clients understanding of annuity and possible perceived biases or preferences.
    - Selling is not only about knowing what to say, but also knowing what not to say.
- Determine investment appetite and risk tolerance.
- Determine stakeholders that need to be in the conversation
- Identify sources of income to fund annuity
- Provide Prospectus and Info on Company
- Talk about 3 Major Concerns (Problem Discovery)
- How can we address those concerns? (Problem Buy-in)
- Ask for Permission to Ask For the Sale
    - If I could put together a strategy that addresses these three main concerns, would you give me 20 minutes to go over some options?

## Stage 3: Product Presentation & Close

After putting together options appropriate to match the client profile/needs we can now present the idea in the context of the client's overall retirement plan. A lot of agents disagree with me and try to have a single meeting as opposed to the old Texas twostep. It's completely up to what's congruent with your style. Personally I don't like coming to a meeting with a specific solution predetermined, it reduces the ability to customize options and make adjustments to your presentation.

- Problem Re-identification (Sum up the last conversation)
- Unveiling the Solution (Present the solution, not the product)
- Check the Rapport
- Ask for the sale
- Submit the Application
- Provide Necessary Prospectus Information

## Stage 4: Follow Up

Follow up is key to success with any sales job. Why? Because, a client has a binary decision to make at the end of any sales presentation. The client can say yes, no or maybe. And like that old country song says, 'Maybe always means no.' Developing a simple follow up strategy could mean the difference between long term success and failure for your life/annuity practice. Any great salesperson will tell you that referrals along with pursuing quotes not taken will fuel your agency growth.

*"If you want truly to understand something, try to change it."* – **Kurt Lewin**

## Chapter 7: Areas of Concerns for Retirees

In this part of the book we are going to cover the three predominant risks facing a client during retirement and leading up to retirement. As personal risk managers we have an obligation and a duty to protect our clients during their golden years. During the distribution phase of retirement the primary concern shifts from growth to sustainability and preservation of capital. So, how do we deliver that preservation of capital and that peace of mind?

### 3 Concerns/Challenges that face every Retired Person

So, what are the three main challenges we all face during retirement? The way I see it, we all face these three very real challenges:

1. You live too long and run out of money.

2. You live too long and get sick or terminally ill.
3. You live too short and run out of savings in a Nursing Facility.

We've addressed some of the monetary concerns earlier in this book. But, the main concerns are overarching concerns in everyone's retirement plan. For instance, what happens if a client works with a financial planner and decides that they need income until age 90. Because, the average life span is 80 years old in America and life expectancy in his family is around average. But, with life extending technology what happens if he lives to 100? No one wants to be the guy who runs out of money.

What happens if you live long but towards the end of your years you become terminally ill and rack up extreme medical debt due to being forced into a nursing home?

What happens if you get seriously injured or sick and rack up bills but then die under the average life expectancy?

These are all situations we never want to think about but insurance is a cost effective way to handle these concerns. Long-term Care built into life insurance is the easiest solution, some annuities even have riders that can help in certain situations.

Median Retirement Savings by Age in the USA

How much time do you have? The average person lives to about 78 or so in the United States. Below is the median distribution of retirement savings in different age brackets, according to a recent Transamerica Study.

- **Americans in their 20s: $16,000**
- **Americans in their 30s: $45,000**
- **Americans in their 40s: $63,000**
- **Americans in their 50s: $117,000**
- **Americans in their 60s: $172,000**

Do you often wonder why people run out of money during retirement? Life happens. Not only does life happen, but illness does not discriminate.

American's have historically low savings and can easily outspend their retirement.

"When a person's interested in something, they're willing to tolerate any kind of problems that may come up." – **Cus D'Amato**

## Chapter 8: 3 Primary Sources of Retirement Income

In this part of the book we're going to breakdown three main sources of retirement income. If one of these three sources of income should collapse and or fail, where does the client retreat to? What does that loss of income imply to the inherent and alteration to the clients lifestyle? What are the implications financially speaking? Historically, these are the three primary sources of retirement income for a typical American.

1. Social Security (Fixed Amount)
2. Qualified Plan / Company Pension
3. Personal Savings

Understand Social Security and potential pitfalls.

Social Security is projected to run deficits by 2032. Which means that we will have more people taking from the system than people putting money into the system for the first time in history. So, what does that mean? It means one of three things happen:

- The government reduces benefits.
- The government increases taxes.
- The government does nothing until the system goes bankrupt.

The Social Security system was created for a limited number of people and expanded over the years. When the system was created the average life span was around 55 years old and is now around 80 years old. When the system was create there were 5 workers paying for a single retiree and now the ratio is about 2:1.

Why Annuities compliment Social Security in a retirement plan.

According to the SSA, '62% of beneficiaries received **AT LEAST HALF** of their income from social security.' Imagine, if you will, a world where social security disappears. Most beneficiaries have limited resources and a fixed income. What's going to be easier for that beneficiary? To suddenly liquidate all assets to make up the lost income or to adjust by having another reliable life time source of income?

## Qualified Plan or Pension Plan

According to a recent study done in the Washington Post, "Only **7 percent** of employers studied offer new employees traditional pensions, which pay out a certain amount at retirement based on a worker's pay and how long they stayed with a company."

Today most Qualified Retirement Plans are usually offered are 401(k) plans. 401(K) plans have limitations as far contribution and distribution of funds. But, overall they are good retirement vehicles. The one big consideration here is how much tax liability does this create and how long can someone live off of their 401k earnings? Unless you have a crystal ball that might be hard to determine.

Why do people have money in their savings account?

Well Mike, because one day I imagine they want to spend it, right? Or to perhaps have a rainy day fund of some kind. Maybe the insured wants to pass one the money to heirs? Maybe the insured would like to slowly liquidate the money. Either they are going to liquidate the money and use it for retirement or they are fearful of some looming unexpected expense. So, I present to you the following question.

What emergency expenses would you need to use your savings for?

Let's assume your insured is retired age 60, with a home that was purchased 30 years ago. The mortgage is most likely paid off. Does a retired person plan on going to college? Probably, not so we can rule out large education expenses. Does the insured plan on buying new expensive cars? Probably, not so we can rule out excessive luxury purchases for the most part. Aside from property taxes what fixed expenses does a person have? Maybe for Medicare Supplement plans and or medication?

So, the most obvious large unexpected expense would be for a nursing home or the cost of in-home nursing care or other non-insurance covered medical expenses. Which is probably the most burdensome and large expense facing our seniors today, that 90% of people never plan for as part of retirement plan.

*"Knowledge comes, but wisdom lingers. It may not be difficult to store up in the mind a vast quantity of facts within a comparatively short time, but the ability to form judgments requires the severe discipline of hard work and the tempering heat of experience and maturity."* **Calvin Coolidge**

## Chapter 9: How Annuities can fill the gap for a retiree.

Annuities can be powerful retirement tools or oversold aggregators of mediocrity. What I mean by that is, when sold in the correct light, as a complementary aspect of retirement plans and not a sole retirement plan, an annuity can be a huge asset to a client's overall portfolio. In this chapter we will discuss how annuities can fill a huge gap in the typical retirement plan that often goes unaddressed until something happens.

### Qualifying Process

1. What part of your retirement is guaranteed?
2. Would you be interested in learning about guaranteed products?
3. What do you like about your current retirement plan?
4. What kind of changes do you want to see in your retirement plan?

5. What is more important to you peace of mind or earnings?
6. Are you the decision maker in your family in regards to financial advising or choosing financial products?
7. Mr. Prospect, you have a significant amount of money saved up in this savings account? What did you plan on doing with it? Why is it there earning negative interest? (Not a literal question)
    a. Well, I want to pass it on to me daughter when I pass away.
    b. What are your investment goals? What your retirement goals? Most people have never taken the time to think about it. Well, at this point I want to not run out of money and leave some behind for my kids and grandkids.
8. What does this client want? What does this client need?
    a. I want to leave money to my family after I pass.
        i. Why is that important to you?

9. Are you happy with the current rate of savings on your savings account or CD?
10. Would you mind if we...
11. How does this sound so far...
12. If I could find a product that has zero risk and guarantees a stream of income for life, would you be open to looking at it?

## Selling Yourself.

How do you build trust? How do you help a customer know, like and trust you? How do you show a customer you care? Start by asking questions but then when you set expectations let them know why you do what you do. What is your reason? What is your story? We all have this yearning to follow people worth following, give them a reason to follow you.

## Analyze Current Retirement Plan

When you analyze a retirement plan remember

although there is a new fiduciary rule in place, you are not technically a fiduciary. Because, you cannot make financial decisions for a client without client consent. A fiduciary is someone who can do that.

What I'm trying to convey is that you should not start trying to reallocate invested funds or money going into investment products. Look for low handing fruit. Look for money sitting in savings accounts. And for E&O purposes make sure you get everything in writing, especially if the client wants to reallocate funds.

Explain/address the Areas of Concern.

This part of the conversation is the, 'what happens if' part of the conversation.

1. You live too long and run out of money.
2. You live too long and get sick or terminally ill.
3. You live too short and run out of savings in a Nursing Facility.

## Fill the Gaps / Design a Plan

As an Agent if you plan on using these two strategies. Ask yourself, does the client have life insurance in place and long term care? If the client has LTC and life insurance go with the indexed/variable approach. If they are more risk adverse go with the variable annuity approach.

But Mike, what if the client does not have Life Insurance and or does not have long term care insurance?

I'm so glad you asked! The answer is the three product close. We fund an immediate annuity, take some of the life time income and distribute that to pay for life insurance and long term care insurance.

Tax Advantages of this strategy?

Long Term Care can be tax deductible up to a certain amount of the premiums depending on the plan. So, check with your CPA and the Client's CPA before executing this strategy with a client based on that information.

### Major Downsides of this plan.

Like any retirement vehicle or part of a retirement plan, there are going to be drawbacks. It's par for the course. Here are three primary concerns:

1. Long term care has an elimination period from 30 to 90 days.
2. Annuities have surrender periods.
3. Life insurance has surrender periods.

*But Mike, if we are selling peace of mind how do we justify the drawbacks?*

There is a price for liquidity and there is a price

for guarantees. There is a price for everything. Remember this is the most stable aspect of a retirement plan. There is not potential for loss and the insurance companies pay into a reinsurance fund protecting up to $250,000 of your money. Much in the same way that the FDIC insures a bank account.

## Case Study Client Example

Let's say you have a healthy couple of health individual with $240,000 in savings earning less than 1% interest. They have their home paid off and low or no credit card debt. You've spent the time to analyse their financial needs and determine that they have no life insurance, they have no long term care insurance and there is a definite need for an annuity.

Let's say after speaking with the client age 60 to 65 we uncover these needs and discover an interest to purchase an annuity. But, we also need to protect against illness or high medical bills due to long term care.

What we can do is take a lump sum of $150,000 to $160,000 in an immediate life-only annuity. So, why would we do this? The customer would have enough saved for emergencies in savings, but would earn more than the interest was paying out on the savings account.

The main reason we would do this is to fund a Long Term Care policy and a GUL. Or find a way to build LTC into the permanent life insurance. There are pros and cons to either option. LTC can be tax deductible up to certain amounts given certain circumstances, but in a life policy is cheaper to purchase. It's cheaper in a life policy because it usually just expiates a death benefit that would have been paid anyways. In a life policy there is no elimination period for LTC. Weigh the pros and cons with each client and go from there.

Let's say we go with the Standalone LTC product. We would purchase a policy with a lifetime benefit of around $170,000 to $180,000 or a monthly benefit of around $5000 to $6000. The premium would be somewhere in the ballpark of $350 per month.

Now how do we pay for the Long Term Care? Simple, the immediate income from the annuity provides a monthly payout factor of around $700 for the life of the annuitant. Now since we are investing a large sum of the client's capital in an annuity and the annuity payments run the length of the annuitant's life we need to hedge our bets. We then place a $150,000 to $160,000 permanent life policy on the client in case they die prematurely. This would be somewhere in the ball park of $200 per month depending on health and product selection.

The net financial result to the client would be 3 products that would cost about $600 per month and leave about $200 per month in excess income. Obviously, these are estimates. The net result to the client's retirement plan is that it protects against premature death. It protects against living too long and fear of running out of money. It protects against a client getting sick and entering a nursing home facility.

What we are doing here is leveraging assets to provide peace of mind and help seniors deal with unforeseen costs during retirement.

### Address Possible Objections

- I heard annuities are bad investments.
    - Why? Just dig. Usually this springs from a CPA or some kind of television personality who has a vested interested in managed funds… But, again don't try to take positions and tell someone they are wrong. Just try to understand and pivot.
- Can't you just give me a quote over the phone?

- o I sure could and I am sure there are lot of Agent who would do just that. This is a real policy and my job is to make sure that I know who I am insuring. But, aside from that it's also my job to make sure we explain the insurance/investment in a way that is easy to understand and answer any questions you might have. (address concerns)
- If I need the money I can't access it.
  - o Liquidity has a price. Much like how accessing money in a 401K before a certain age results in an extra tax penalty.
- If I die tomorrow the life insurance company keeps everything?
  - o This is why we purchase the life insurance with part of the income provided by the annuity.

Building a Fact Finder

After working with thousands of Agents let me tell you, I've seen some great fact finding sheets and some that could use improvement. Fact finding sheets to me are essential to keeping a consistent process. Here are some of the questions and topics you should always address in a fact finding sheet.

Fact finding sheets should have some literal questions and some underpinning questions that are the subtext of conversation. For instance, the fact finding sheet should help you understand client goals, and determine a compelling vision for the future. Fact finding sheets should help you understand why the person is sitting down and giving you the time of day. They should help provide clarity about expectations and a client's understanding of their own financial needs.

1. Determine number, let the client tell you how much they plan on living on during retirement. It has to be there number.

2. Having a commitment on the fact finding sheet prior to the proposal stage. Not a financial commitment but a commitment of will to go through the presentation. "I John Snow, request the projected amount of money needed during my retirement, assuming I want to retire at age 65..."
3. Current Life Insurance
    a. Amount of Insurances
    b. Company
    c. Premium
4. Current Liquid Assets
    a. Cash
    b. Stocks & investments
5. Current Non-liquid Assets
    a. Home, boat, auto, etc.
6. Current Income
    a. Job Type
    b. Length of Employment
7. Spouses Current Income
    a. Same as above.
8. Beneficiary
    a. Spouse? Child? Charity?
9. Employer Name

10. Vacation Time, if still working.
11. Projected Retirement Date or Age
    a. Working during retirement?
12. Existing Pension Plan?
13. Tobacco User?
14. Money needed to retire? Goals? Amount of money during?

## Pro's and Cons of Annuities

As a consultant now looking as an outsider it's quite bizarre to me that annuities can be so polarizing. Either someone is 100% on board with the concept or 100% against ever even considering the validity of an annuity strategy. Typically, people overstate the value and understate the risk of an annuity, like most insurance products. Insurance in my humble opinion is the most powerful social good ever created and for a financially conservative minded client can add tremendous value by way of financial stability and overall peace of mind.

## The Argument for Annuities

**Lifetime Income** – with an immediate annuity we are getting the client a guaranteed periodic payment as long as they live. The insurance company is taking a risk some people die soon and some live long.

**Inflation Protection** – Annuities have inflation riders much like other life insurance products to keep pace with inflation. There is a high degree of customization in the annuity market.

**Principal Protection** – If we go with the Indexed Annuity then the principal is protected against any loss, because we cap the gain and the insurance company keeps the difference.

## The Argument against Annuities

**Lower Returns on Your Investment** – The tradeoff for an annuity is capital growth potential. We are limited by growth and shrinkage. Protection comes at a cost.

**High Costs:** Some annuities offer a 10% commission and high management fees which can eat away at gains or lower the ceiling for some products.

**Inflexible** – Annuities like all retirement vehicles are meant for long term growth potential and thus are inflexible to some extent.

"Wisdom is the reward you get for a lifetime of listening when you'd have preferred to talk." -- Doug Larson

# Chapter 10: Dealing with External Stakeholders

Since the dawn of time insurance agents have had to deal with client's saying, "Let me speak with my lawyer." We've all heard it before. When dealing with stakeholders we can either take a combative approach, "I know best, because I'm the insurance guy and he is the accountant." Or we can choose to take the cooperative role, "We're on the same side, the side of the client."

## The Triple A's

There are three key stakeholders that your insurance will take more serious than your 40 years selling insurance. I call these the 'Triple A's' of stakeholders.

- Accountants
- Advisors
- Attorneys

Each stakeholder is in a way the same but

different. Each stakeholder has a preconceived notion as to what insurance is meant for. Why? Because, they all have insurance and different experiences with insurance. So, what does that mean for us insurance agents? It means that we have a unique opportunity to be different.

What do most Agents make the mistake of doing when dealing with a 'Triple A' objection from a client? They almost always instinctively try to dissuade the client from speaking with their representative, which in the clients mind does what? It almost surely confirms the client's initial gut reaction to confer with their advisor.

"I need to speak with my husband/wife/spouse."

This is a fairly straight forward yet difficult objection to overcome, why? Because, if you challenge the insured you are undermining their care for their loved ones. So, where did we go wrong?

Why did the client present this objection? Why? Because, we didn't ask ahead of time. When selling annuities I could be asking you to move $500,000 in funds into an agreement with no surrender options. It's likely that the insured would like to consult a spouse! So, just ask during your qualifying process. Are you the one who would normally make these decisions? Do you normally make these kind of decisions or do you consult with someone else?

### Flipping the Script

So, how do you get a thoroughly entrenched financial advisor to switch their stance on annuities and life insurance? The answer is you need to set boundaries and not try to act like a retirement planner or certified financial advisor. Our job is risk management and we do this by hedging against life events that could financially devastate a client. Our job is not to destroy the years of work the advisor did to build the estate up, not is it to compete dollar for dollar. Our job is to compliment and restructure parts of the plan in a way that will protect the client from risk.

How long can you guarantee our client will live to? What's the date? The answer we don't know. Most people live to the ripe old age of 78, but if you're in my family that number could be as high as 106 years old. Is the client going to immune to health issues? Do people become healthier or less healthy as we age? What are the odds the person needs disability coverage or nursing home care? What should that level of care look like? Is it important to you as an advisor that our client doesn't need to immediately liquidate their portfolio to pay for nursing home care? What if they need 24/7 in home care?

As our client's financial advisor, when do they plan on retiring? Let's say they plan on retiring at age 70. Great, now how much money will they need to live out their retirement? Well... The answer is neither of us can say with 100% certainty and we do claim to know then we are lying to ourselves and the client. Why do we not know? Because, life happens. What if they need to relocate? What if they become critically ill? What if taxes go up? What if social security fails? All I can say is that with an immediate annuity I can guarantee that our client will never out live the stream of income.

Ultimately, we're all salespeople. So, sell them on you, sell them on your concept and sell them on annuities. You know you've got this down when you can turn a skeptical stakeholder into a referral partner.

"To keep everyone invested in your vision, you have to back up a little bit and really analyze who the different stakeholders are and what they individually respond to." Alan Stern

## Chapter 11: Understanding Stats

I've always felt that a great salesperson is a great educator. As part of being an educator we must first become highly educated, in theory. There are a lot of interesting statistics that will help you sell insurance, more so help you get people thinking about why to buy insurance. Did you know that about 75% of all statistics are made up on the spot? Crazy, right? Insurance humor aside, we can get people thinking quite easily with some of the below talking points and factoids.

- What is the average life need?
- How long do people live?
- What percentage of families are sandwiched families?
- What is the average death benefit?
- What is the average amount of debt?
- What is the average income of a retiree?
- What does the average American retire with?

## Life Statistics

According to a recent study the overall longevity of developed countries is progressively increasing over the last twenty years. (Average Life Span Expectancy Chart - How Long Will I Live - *Disabled World - (2015-02-09))*

- UK: 80 years in 2002, 81.73 years in 2010
- USA: 77.4 years in 2002, 78.24 years in 2010
- Italy: 79.25 years in 2002, 80.33 years in 2010
- Spain: 79.06 years in 2002, 81.07 years in 2010
- Australia: 80 years in 2002, 81.72 years in 2010
- France: 79.05 years in 2002, 81.09 years in 2010
- Monaco: 79.12 years in 2002, 89.73 years in 2011
- Germany: 77.78 years in 2002, 79.41 years in 2010

# Retirement Statistics

According to Rebecca Lake in her article, 'What Are the Retirement Statistics?' here are some of the important stats to know for retirement. Warning some of these may be quite alarming.

- The mean retirement savings of working households aged 32 to 61 is $95,776, according to the Economic Policy Institute.

- Thirty-five percent of workers have $100,000 or more saved for retirement. Thirty-eight percent have less than $10,000 saved

- Fifty-seven percent of workers say saving for retirement is their top financial priority

- Fifty-nine percent of workers expect their standard of living to stay the same or increase in retirement.

- Twenty-four percent of pre-retirees say they'll need $1 million or more to have a secure retirement.

- Twenty percent of workers say they'll never be able to retire.

- Fifty-four percent of pre-retirees say they have no clue how much money they'll need when they retire.

Understanding statistics can be a great way to develop talking points. Not all statistics are useful and created equal. Take the time to find out what statistics might be important to your target demographic.

## Disclaimer

Thanks for taking the time to read this book. Annuities have a lot of potential pitfalls and a lot of potential benefits. It's really going to depend on the individual situation of the client. This information doesn't work in a vacuum and requires a tremendous amount of practice to execute effectively. If you intend on selling to senior's then I urge you to read all of the model regulations in regards to disclosures and requirements for selling to seniors. Selling any annuity qualifies an agent to be considered a fiduciary, so read the new fiduciary rules and understand them thoroughly. Also, before ever considering moving assets out of qualified accounts into annuity products, make sure to consult an attorney, the Third Party Administrator, the client's Human Resources division and a CPA/Accountant. Anytime we as agents advise a client to move large sums of money it does open up the possibility of E&O claims, so make sure you get everything in writing and follow appropriate DOI recommended procedures for selling annuities.

## Index of Questions

- Would it surprise you to know that about half of my clients pay nothing out of pocket for their long term care insurance needs?
- Do you have any other assets that you plan on passing on?
- Do you have anything else that works like life insurance? In that it passes on.
- Would it be fair to say that you've worked your entire life to build this nest egg?
    - Would it also be fair to say that now might be the time you want make sure and protect it the most?
        - Why don't we insure it and lock in those gains?
- What can you tell me about your current retirement plan?
- What is your plan?
    - 'Well I have a 401k'
        - Great. What is the plan?
            - 'What do you mean?

- How do you plan on taking out the money?
- How much? What increments? Did you have a plan that protects you against the market dropping 50%?

## Summation

I hope you enjoyed this book as much as I enjoyed writing it for you, and when I say for you, I mean it. I'm not planning on retiring on a $5 book that I split a small percentage with the publisher. This book was written to help you develop your life practice. I'm a strong believer that the perennial student is the richest person on earth. We are in the golden ages of annuity sales, we are seeing the first wave of baby boomers retiring, all the while picking up the pieces 10 years later after the 'great recession'. This in my estimation provides a tremendous amount of opportunity for annuity sales, because the next recession could be right around the corner. With the looming threat of tariffs and trade wars upending the global ecosystem, it might be the right time for many Americans to consider protecting what they have saved so hard for all these years.

www.ingramcontent.com/pod-product-compliance
Lightning Source LLC
Chambersburg PA
CBHW030719220526
45463CB00005B/2113